BLESSED BY GOD
MARILYN TRUELUCK
No part of this book may be copied, reproduced or sold without express permission from the owner.
copyright ALPHA ZURIEL PUBLISHING © 2022. All rights reserved

Thank You, God, for all You do
For the sun that shines and the sky so blue

For the birds that sing and the flowers that
bloom
For the love You give, it fills up this room

Thank You, God, for the food we eat

*For the clothes we wear
and the bed we sleep*

For the people we love and the friends we make
For all the blessings You give, for goodness sake

*Thank You, God, for the world
we live
For the mountains and rivers,
the sand and the sieve*

For the animals big and small
For it all, we stand up tall

Thank You, God, for the shining stars
For the moon that glows and the planets
that are

For the oceans so deep and the mountains so high
For the beauty in nature, we look to the sky

Thank You, God, for the wonders of life
For the joy and the laughter, the love and the
strife

For the struggles we face and the lessons we learn
For the journey ahead, You guide us in turn

Thank You, God, for the hope that You bring
For the peace in Your presence, the love You sing

*For the promise of forever and the comfort
of home
For the grace that You give, we are never
alone*

Thank You, God, for Your endless grace
For Your mercy and kindness, Your love we embrace
For all You've given us, we are so blessed
Thank You, God, for Your endless rest